D1126755

# Busy Machines

by DAVID L. HARRISON
illustrated by RICHARD WALZ

A GOLDEN BOOK • NEW YORK
Western Publishing Company, Inc., Racine, Wisconsin 53404

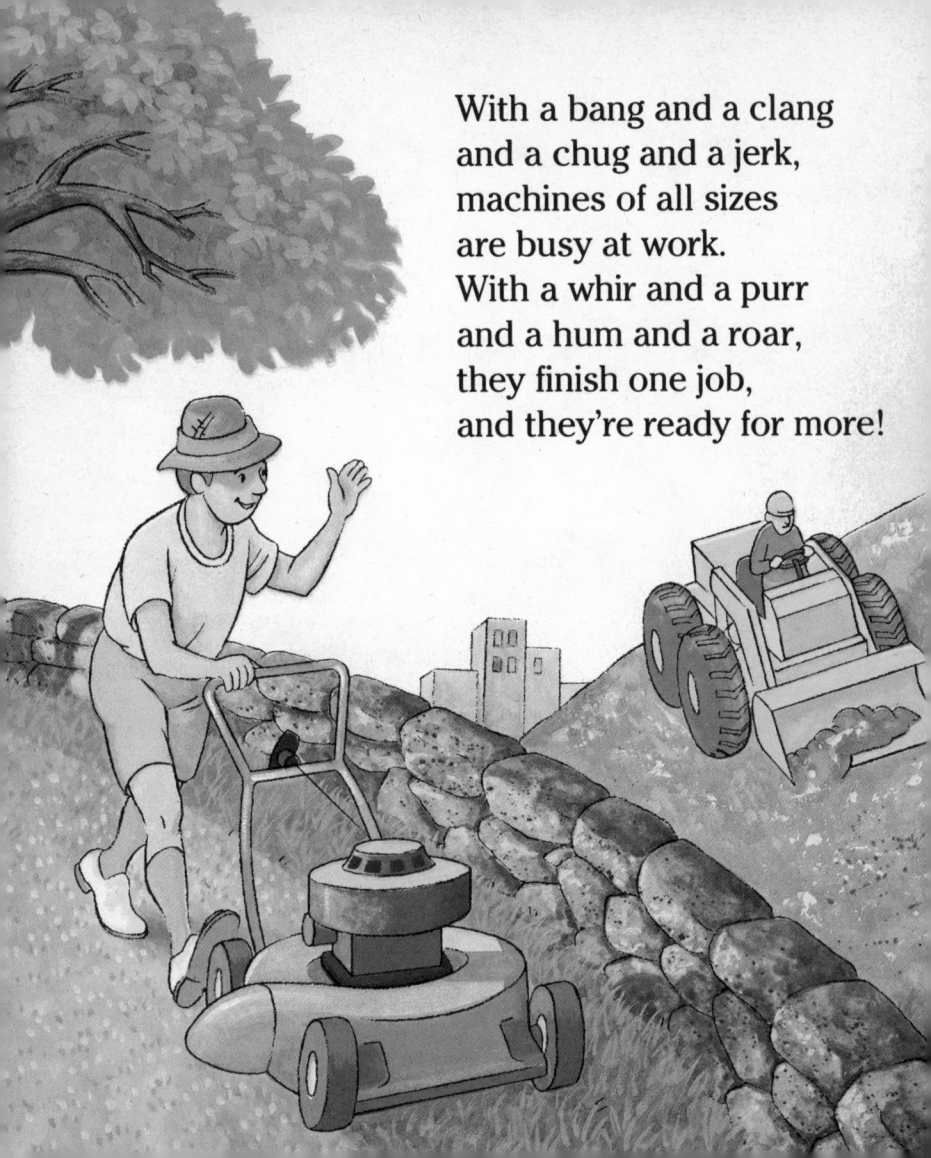

With a bang and a clang
and a chug and a jerk,
machines of all sizes
are busy at work.
With a whir and a purr
and a hum and a roar,
they finish one job,
and they're ready for more!

The DRILLER drills
a new well.
Well, well!
Might find water,
cool to drink.
Might find oil,
black as ink.
Might find nothing!
What do you think?
Well, well!

Up and down
the farmer's fields
the TRACTOR goes,
pulling plows
and planting what
the farmer grows.
And when they're done
the crops will grow
in even rows.

The LOG SLASHER sounds like a thousand bumblebees as it buzzes in the forest sawing trees.

The road is like
a concrete ribbon
after the PAVER is through.
No lumps or bumps
or holes or humps.
The road is smooth
and fresh and new
after the PAVER is through.

CRUSHERS crush rocks
and smash rocks
and squash rocks
and mash rocks
and crunch rocks
and bash rocks
and crack rocks
and thrash rocks.
CRUSHERS are just plain
hard on rocks.

That giraffe
may think he's tall,
but next to an AERIAL LIFT
he's small.
Need to reach
above the trees?
An AERIAL LIFT can do it
with ease.

What eats grass
with a hungry roar?
A MOWER.
So whatever kind of
grass you're growing—
get mowing!

A LOADER lifts a lot of loads
and dumps them into dump trucks.
Push and pile and scrape and scoop
and load another dump truck.
Need to load a load?
Call a LOADER!

How do people set a steeple?
With a CRANE.
Raise a tower in an hour?
With a CRANE.
Lift the engine of a train?
Set a farmer's weather vane?
Set a silo for the grain?
With a CRANE!

A SPRAYER is
the fastest way
for folks who have
a lot to spray
and want to have
some time to play.

What do LIFT TRUCKS lift?
Railroad tracks and railroad ties.
Boxes, blocks, and frozen pies.
Lumber, barrels, cartons, bricks,
cages full of cheeping chicks.
Anything you need to lift,
that's what LIFT TRUCKS lift.

The ROLLER irons the road smooth
and presses out its wrinkles.
The road looks like
it's come from the cleaners
after the ROLLER rolls by.

A DOZER pulls up a tree,
knocks down a shed,
and scrapes away brush
so a fire doesn't spread.
It's steam-engine noisy
and elephant strong.
It's rough and it's tough!
That's what a DOZER is.

A CAR CRUSHER
crushes cars
until they're flat.
Think of that!
It seems to like
to gobble cars
for lunch.
Crunch! Crunch!

Bit by bit
and inch by inch,
the TRENCHER saws
and gnaws a trench.

Nothing digs a hole
like a BACKHOE can.
Deep holes, steep holes,
more-than-you-can-leap holes.
Need to dig a hole?
Call a BACKHOE man.

When the winter
blizzards blow,
the SNOW PLOW shoves
and scrapes the snow
so all the cars
and trucks can go.

The FELLER BUNCHER
grabs a tree
and whacks it right in two!
I think
a FELLER BUNCHER's strong!
Don't you?

Blade away and grade away,
scrape and cut and shave away,
any way to smooth a way,
that's the GRADER's way.

If a farmer has a BALER,
he can build a bale of hay.
If he gets a bigger BALER
he can build a bigger bale.
But does a bigger bale
build a bigger cow?
Don't ask the farmer.
He's busy now.

The farmer's through farming
and all over town,
the workers have shut their machinery down.
They've turned off the loader
and switched off its light.

The pavers and dozers are parked for the night.
But wait till tomorrow,
and then with a roar,
those busy machines will get busy once more!

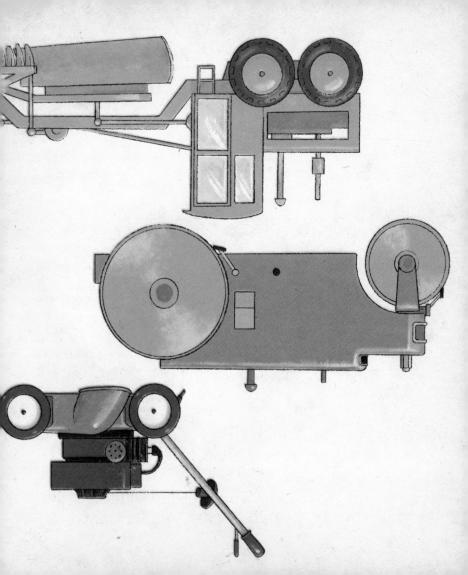